Shabu Shabu Recipes

Recipes

A Complete Cookbook of Japanese

Dish Ideas!

Table of Contents

Introduction

How can you integrate shabu shabu foods into your recipe repertoire at home?

Can you seek out the different varieties of ingredients you'll need to make these dishes?

Are you curious about the various ways in which Japanese foods can make your recipes tastier?

Shabu shabu is different from other Japanese hot pot recipes is that you won't be simmering everything before the meal is served. Instead, you will prepare the broth and then dip in the vegetables and meat to cook them, before dipping them in tasty sauces to enjoy.

In this cookbook, you'll discover how to use Japanese foods in 30 different shabu shabu dishes.

Read on and try out some of these tasty recipes. You may even find more dishes that can benefit from the inclusion of ingredients from the Japanese taste palate.

1 – Favorite Shabu Shabu Sauces

These are the most commonly used dipping sauces for shabu shabu meals. They are easy to make, and they create a wonderful taste sensation when combined with the freshly cooked meats and vegetables.

Ponzu Sauce

Ingredients

- 1/2 tsp. of fresh ginger, grated
- 1 1/2 cups of water, filtered
- 1/4 cup vinegar
- 1/2 cup soy sauce (shoyu), low sodium

- 1/2 cup lemon juice, fresh

Instructions

Combine the ingredients in each sauce. Prepare and set aside for dipping.

Sesame Sauce

Ingredients

- 2 cups water, purified
- 1/2 cup soy sauce (shoyu), low sodium
- 1/3 cup Tahini
- 1 tbsp. mustard
- 1/4 cup sake
- 1/2 cup vinegar, rice
- 1/3 cup mirin
- 1/4 cup sugar, granulated
- 1/4 cup miso

- 1/3 cup ground sesame seeds, toasted

Instructions

Combine the ingredients in each sauce. Prepare and set aside for dipping.

Garlic Sauce

Ingredients

- 1/4 cup oil, canola
- 1 tsp. salt, kosher
- 1/4 cup lemon juice, fresh
- 1/4 cup garlic, minced

Instructions

Combine the ingredients in each sauce. Prepare and set aside for dipping.

Teriyaki Sauce

Ingredients

- 4 to 5 tbsp. honey, pure
- 1 tbsp. corn starch
- 1/2 cup water, filtered
- 1/4 cup soy sauce, reduced sodium

Instructions

Combine the ingredients in each sauce. Prepare and set aside for dipping. These recipes make extra, because you'll probably need it.

2 – Kimchi Pork Shabu Shabu

This is a comforting, warm kimchi pork belly stew that is filled with veggies and pork. It's perfect for winter dinners during the week or to be savored over the extra time allowed at weekend dinners.

Makes 4 Servings

Cooking + Prep Time: 2 hours and 35 minutes

Ingredients:

- 2 or 3 chunked potatoes
- 1 to 2 cups of mushrooms, sliced
- 1 sliced carrot

- 1 to 2 tbsp. of mirin
- 2 cups of kimchi, including juice
- 1 sliced onion
- Sea salt black pepper
- 1 lb. of pork belly slab, with skin removed
- Bread, pasta or noodles, as desired
- For garnishing: green onions, sliced
- Your choice of dipping sauces – (see recipe 1)

Instructions:

1. Slice pork belly into cubes of 1-inch square. Season with salt pepper on all sides.

2. Heat up pot on med-high. Sear belly on all sides until brown and golden. Remove pork from pan. Set aside.

3. Add sliced onions. Cook on med. heat 'til they are soft and brown.

4. Add mushrooms, kimchi and carrots. Brown them lightly.

5. Add pork back to pot. Combine well. Add water sufficient to cover pork just barely. Bring to slow simmer.

6. Cover pan. Simmer stew for about an hour. Stir in potatoes.

7. Cover. Continue cooking for one more hour. Pork should be very tender.

8. Add mirin. Season using salt pepper if desired. Sprinkle with green onions.

9. Enjoy with bread, pasta or noodles and dipping sauces - see recipe 1.

3 – Mushroom Kombu Shabu Shabu

Shabu shabu is not served as often as other Japanese dishes in restaurants, because it needs a table heating source. It is cooked in many homes, though. You can select vegetables from your garden or refrigerator if you like. Most of the food can be prepared ahead of time and then removed from the fridge when you're ready for the dinner.

Makes 2-4 Servings

Cooking + Prep Time: 1 hour and 10 minutes

Ingredients:

- 4 green onions, washed cubed
- 2 pkgs. of tofu, soft, washed and diced
- 8 oz. of chrysanthemum, only leaves
- 8 oz. of washed trimmed watercress
- 2 pkgs. of washed enokitake (white mushrooms), fresh, with ends removed
- 4 matsutake (spicy mushrooms), fresh
- 8 sliced in wedges shiitake mushrooms, fresh
- 3 cleaned, cut leeks
- 4 leaves of cleaned, sliced cabbage, Chinese
- 1 1/2 lbs. of cut beef, sliced thinly
- 1 dash of soy sauce, white
- 1/2 sheet of kombu (kelp), dried
- Dipping sauces, your choice – see recipe 1

Instructions:

1. Set up fondue pot on the table.

2. Fill the pot 3/4 full of water. Add dash soy sauce and kombu. Allow to sit as broth for an hour before you cook.

3. Cut arrange dipping ingredients on platter on table.

4. Remove kombu from broth. Turn the burner on under pot. Keep the heat at medium while you cook, so that no water boils away.

5. When water becomes hot, dip individual slices of meat in broth. Swish it around until the meat darkens. This only takes from 5-15 seconds. Remove. Dip into sauces.

6. Drop veggies into broth. Allow to sit until done, usually around one minute. Dip into sauces.

4 – Vegetable Lamb Shabu Shabu

Shabu shabu is a new use for your fondue pot. The fresh vegetables and thinly sliced lamb cook in the flavorful, hot kombu broth, right at your table. You can purchase sliver-thin sliced meats at Asian grocery or meat stores or local butcher shops, or slice them yourself.

Makes 8 Servings

Cooking + Prep Time: 2 hours

Ingredients:

For kombu broth

- 1 oz. of kombu
- 12 cups of water, cold
- 2 tsp. of salt, kosher

For Shabu Shabu

- 4 cups of white rice, long-grain, cooked, hot
- 1 x 8-oz. peeled sliced lotus root
- 6 oz. of enoki mushrooms
- 6 oz. of shiitake mushrooms, caps only
- 8 oz. of snow peas
- 7 oz. of halved baby Bok choy
- 8 oz. of corn ears, baby
- 2 x 12-oz. rib eyes, boneless

For dipping – see recipe 1

- Ponzu sauce
- Garlic sauce

Instructions:

1. To make kombu broth, combine 12 cups of cold water kombu in large sized pot. Cover. Bring to boil on high heat. Remove as soon as it boils. Allow to stand for about 15 minutes. Discard the kombu.

2. Stir in 2 tsp. of salt. Bring to slow simmer on medium heat.

3. Pour remaining broth in heated large fondue pot.

4. Serve veggies and beef alongside, to dip.

5. Cook veggies in broth until they are tender but crisp.

6. Cook the beef in broth to your preferred doneness level, 5-15 seconds.

7. Serve with ponzu and garlic sauce, plus rice, if desired.

5 – Tofu Beef Shabu Shabu

This recipe joins beef and tofu together to allow you to take advantage of the wonderful tastes mingling. You can use your favorite vegetables in lieu of those below, and any other seasonal ingredients you like.

Makes 2 Servings

Cooking + Prep Time: 35 minutes

Ingredients:

- 8 carrots sliced into flowers
- 1 sliced scallion, Japanese

- 6 shiitake mushrooms with removed stalks
- 3 1/2 inches of trimmed enoki mushrooms
- 1 handful shingiku (chrysanthemums)
- Several bite-sized cut Napa cabbage leaves
- 5 1/3 oz. of square cut tofu, firm
- 1 pc. of cut kombu (kelp)
- Water, hot
- Dashi soup base
- 7 ounces of beef, sliced thinly

Dipping Sauces – see recipe 1

- Sesame dipping sauce
- Ponzu dipping sauce

Instructions:

1. Prepare the vegetables. Arrange on platter. Prepare the dipping sauces (see recipe 1). Divide in 2 portions.

2. Soak kelp in pot of hot water for about 15 minutes. Bring water in pot to simmer, then turn heat off. Discard the kelp.

3. Briefly dip beef slices in soup base. Cook veggies in soup base, as well. Dip in sauces.

6 – Veggie Shabu Shabu

Contrary to what you may have read, you don't need a meat to make this dish delicious. When you have a flavorful broth as your cooking method, you can use vegetables to create a wonderful meatless meal.

Makes 2 Servings

Cooking + Prep Time: 1 hour 40 minutes

Ingredients:

- Vegetable broth
- 1 tbsp. of miso paste
- 3 tbsp. of kochujang (hot pepper paste)
- 2 pcs. of ginger, fresh

- 1 stalk of celery
- 2 medium carrots
- 1 onion

Instructions:

1. Start vegetable broth in large pot. Bring to boil for about five minutes. Add in ginger, celery, onions and carrots.

2. Simmer over med. heat, covered, for 1/2 hour or so.

3. Add kochujang paste and miso. Simmer over med-low for an hour or so. Season using salt pepper, as desired.

4. Cut up some more veggies of choice, prepare table with sliced meat, noodles, tofu, etc.

5. Dip veggies, meat and noodles in hot broth to cook. Use dipping sauce (see recipe 1) as desired.

7 – Bok Choy Cabbage Shabu Shabu

Shabu shabu is easy to make at home, since the prep is simple and it will tempt you deliciously. You'll also enjoy shabu shabu because it's light, so it fills you up in a warm and comforting way.

Makes 2-4 Servings

Cooking + Prep Time: 55 minutes

Ingredients:

- Green onions, chopped
- Daikon, grated
- 1 pkg. of udon or ramen noodles
- 2 pounds of thinly sliced beef

- 2 cups of mushrooms
- 1 pkg. of enoki mushrooms
- 10 quartered baby Bok choy
- 2 large Korean green onions
- 1/2 head of 2-inch cut Napa cabbage
- 2 bags of dashi
- Dipping sauces (see recipe 1)

Sesame dressing

- Ponzu

Instructions:

1. Add 8 cups of water and 2 bags of dashi to large pot. Bring to boil and allow to simmer for about 15 minutes.

2. Prepare veggies and sauces (see recipe 1).

3. Arrange ingredients on plates.

4. Set burner for pot. Place ingredients on the table.

5. Give guests a plate or bowl for food, two dishes for sauces and forks or chopsticks.

6. Bring broth pot to table. Set on burner. Bring to simmer. Add vegetables. Allow guests to cook meat in broth. It takes only 5-10 seconds on average.

7. Dip veggies and meat in dipping sauces.

8 – Tamari Beef Shabu Shabu

This is a traditional beef recipe that takes popular Japanese foods and turns them into savory, delicious soup. This Asian soup turns out so delicious, you'll enjoy it often.

Makes 2-4 Servings

Cooking + Prep Time: 20 min.

Ingredients:

- 10 leaves chopped Thai basil
- 1 cup bean sprouts
- 20 leaves whole Thai basil
- 1 lb. tenderloin, beef, sliced very thinly
- 2 tbsp. hoisin sauce
- 4 1/2 cups stock, chicken
- 1/4 cup tamari
- 1/2 cup lime juice, fresh
- 2 fresh limes, halved
- 2 tbsp. marmalade, orange
- 2 tsp. fresh garlic, minced
- 2 tbsp. fresh ginger, shredded
- 2 tbsp. oil, olive
- Sea salt ground pepper, as desired

Instructions:

1. Warm the oil on low heat in medium pan.

2. Add garlic and ginger. Sauté until they are fragrant.

3. Stir in the orange marmalade, plus hoisin sauce, chicken stock, tamari and 1/4 cup of lime juice. Raise heat to med-high. Cook for 10 minutes and season as desired.

4. Pile the slices of beef in soup bowls.

5. Heat the broth in pot until boiling hot. Add the other 1/4 cup of lime juice, along with chopped basil. Fill the bowls with broth.

6. Serve with lime halves and dipping sauce (see recipe 1).

9 – Shrimp Dumpling Shabu Shabu

This recipe uses dumplings and shrimp to give you the Japanese taste you love. You can use tofu as well, if you like. Experiment with different vegetables and protein sources and discover your favorite meals.

Makes 4-6 Servings

Cooking + Prep Time: 40 minutes

Ingredients:

- 2 cups of chopped mushrooms, fresh
- 2 cups of Bok choy, chopped
- 7 oz. of noodles, udon
- 4 pot stickers, frozen
- 8 de-shelled and de-veined shrimps, fresh
- 1/8 tsp. of peppercorns, whole
- 3 or 4 chopped chili peppers, dried
- 3 to 4 star anise
- 1 tbsp. of soy sauce, low sodium
- 3 garlic cloves, whole
- 8 cups of vegetable broth
- 1 diced white onion, sweet, large
- Optional garnish: chopped cilantro, fresh

Instructions:

1. Sauté the onion in fry pan until it caramelizes.

2. Add spices, stock and garlic to large pot. Simmer for about 20 minutes.

3. Add pot stickers and pasta. Boil for 6-8 minutes.

4. Add veggies and shrimp. Boil for three minutes.

5. Ladle the soup into bowls.

6. Lay out trays of meat and veggies to be cooked.

7. Serve with dipping sauces (see recipe 1).

10 – Sirloin Bell Pepper Shabu Shabu

Shabu shabu is like a fondue, with its flavor-infused broth. It's much healthier than fondue, too, since it's not as thick. The broth is the key. Make sure it is of high quality, or make it yourself.

Makes 4 Servings

Cooking + Prep Time: 35 minutes

Ingredients:

- 1 tbsp. of cilantro, chopped
- 1/2 trimmed bunch of green onions

- 1/2 cup of shiitake mushrooms with discarded stems
- 1/2 cup of sliced carrots
- 1 sliced bell pepper
- 1 cup of shredded Napa cabbage
- 1/2 pound of firm tofu
- 1 1/2 pounds of sliced sirloin steaks
- 4 cups of broth, chicken

For dipping (see recipe 1)

- Teriyaki sauce
- Sesame sauce
- Ponzu sauce

Instructions:

1. Bring broth to boil in large sized pot.

2. Arrange beef slices on platter.

3. Arrange veggies on another platter.

4. Transfer broth to hot pot or fondue pot on table. Add cilantro. Use the fondue forks for dipping food in simmering broth. Serve with sauces.

11 – Seaweed Udon Shabu Shabu

This dish offers a fantastic time cooking your ingredients and eating them, too, in a hot pot shabu shabu recipe. This cuisine is a tasty and sociable hot pot meal that allows you to swish the ingredients in boiling broth to cook them. It's made unforgettable by the wonderful tastes of the dipping sauces.

Makes 4 Servings

Cooking + Prep Time: 50 minutes

Ingredients:

- 1/2 head of cabbage, Chinese
- 2 medium carrots
- 1 pkg. of shiitake or enoki mushrooms
- 10 1/2 oz. of beef, sliced thinly
- 1 pack of tofu
- 4 packages of udon noodles, fresh
- 1 pack of kombu seaweed, dried
- Ponzu dipping sauce (see recipe 1)

Instructions:

1. Fill large pot on dinner table 2/3 full of boiling water. Add kombu and allow to soak for about 1/2 an hour.

2. Cut up veggies and meat into thin slices. Then cut tofu into small-sized cubes.

3. Return kombu to boil on stove. Remove it when water starts to boil. Set on hot pad on table.

4. Have guests or family use long forks to stir tofu, meat and veggies in broth until they are cooked.

5. Dip in dipping sauces (see recipe 1).

6. After veggies and meat have cooked, add udon noodles into pot for a few minutes to soak up the remaining delicious flavors. Finish your meal with the tasty noodles.

12 – Bok Choy Beef Shabu Shabu

This recipe is fun for children and children at heart. Everyone gets to sit around the boiling pot of broth, cooking their veggies and meat. The plates of vegetables arrive first, followed by thinly sliced meats, which don't take as long to cook.

Makes 4-6 Servings

Cooking + Prep Time: 55 minutes

Ingredients:

For broth

- 3 shiitake mushrooms, dried
- 5 x 5" seaweed, kombu

For vegetables meat

- 1 pkg. of udon or ramen noodles
- 2 lbs. of chicken, pork or beef, sliced thinly
- 2 cups of mushrooms
- 1 pkg. of enoki mushrooms with trimmed ends
- 10 quartered baby Bok choy
- 1 bundle of yu chou (like Bok choy) with trimmed ends
- 2 sliced green onions
- 1/2 head of cut Napa cabbage

Instructions:

1. Add kombu and 8 cups of water to large bowl and leave to soak for 1/2 hour. Pour this water into large-sized pot.

2. Add mushrooms. Bring to boil. Remove kombu. Simmer for about 15 minutes.

3. Prepare veggies and meats. Arrange ingredients on plates.

4. Set up portable burner. Have guests use plate or bowl of food, chopsticks and two dishes of dipping sauces (see recipe 1).

5. Bring broth pot to table. Set on portable burner. Bring to simmer. Add veggies that take longest to cook. While they cook, guests may start cooking meat by dipping it in the simmering broth. The meat will cook within seconds.

6. Dip veggies and meat into dipping sauces.

13 – Turnip Mushroom Shabu Shabu

This is an easy Japanese hot pot dish you can make at home. Shabu shabu with pork and mushrooms is perfect, especially for cold weather. Your whole family will love it.

Makes 6 Servings

Cooking + Prep Time: 45 minutes

Ingredients:

For the dashi

- 1 cup of bonito flakes
- 4 oz. of kombu
- 12 cups of water

For the shabu shabu

- 2 chopped purple turnips, medium
- 3 halved Vidalia onions
- 1 1/2 cups of stemmed shiitake mushrooms
- 1/2 cup of trimmed enoki mushrooms
- 3 washed heads of Bok choy with separated leaves
- 2 chopped cups of mizuna (Asian greens)
- 1 lb. of thinly sliced pork loin
- 1 lb. of thinly sliced rib-eye
- 3 x 8-oz. pkgs. of udon noodles – boil until they are tender, then drain and rinse in cold water
- 1 x 14-oz. pkg. of cubed tofu, firm

Instructions:

1. To make dashi, combine kombu and water in sauce pan on med-high. Bring to simmer. Cook for about 15 minutes. Stir in bonito flakes. Cook for five more minutes.

2. Remove pan from heat. Strain dashi and discard solids.

3. To prepare the shabu shabu, arrange meats on platter and tofu and veggies on another. Place cooked noodles in a large bowl.

4. Set your portable stove on dining table. Place ceramic pot on burner. Pour strained dashi in the pot. Cover. Bring to simmer.

5. As dashi is warming, bring noodles, meat and veggies to table.

6. Have guests work in batches to cook veggies and meat. Dip cooked veggies and meat in sauces (see recipe 1).

14 – Beef Veggie Shabu Shabu

This traditional shabu shabu recipe is quick and easy, with its veggies, meat and broth – and don't forget the dipping sauces. It's like Asian fast food only better.

Makes 8 Servings

Cooking + Prep Time: 25 minutes

Ingredients:

- 2 pounds of 1-inch cubed tofu, pressed, drained
- 1 pound of watercress
- 2 pounds of cabbage, Chinese

- 1 pound of shirataki pasta
- 1 pound of shimeji mushrooms
- 1 pound of enoki mushrooms
- 16 shiitake mushrooms
- 6 slices of kombu
- 2 pounds of thinly sliced beef

Instructions:

1. Place a few slices of the kombu kelp in medium pot. Use cold water to cover.

2. Bring water slowly to boil. Remove kombu before it starts boiling. Let water boil gently.

3. Pour hot broth in fondue pot on table. Arrange meat and veggies on platters.

4. Take meat or veggie, and swish it around in hot water. Several seconds will do for the beef and several minutes for the veggies.

5. Serve with steamed rice and dipping sauces (see recipe 1).

15 – Kombu Brisket Shabu Shabu

Kombu can be purchased in folded packages, and it folds out to about three to four inches after you soak it. The sesame dipping sauce can be joined by ponzu sauce and red chili paste, if you like.

Makes 8 Servings

Cooking + Prep Time: 1 hour 10 minutes

Ingredients:

For dashi broth

- 5 tbsp. of miso paste, white or light
- 10 shiitake caps, dried
- 3 to 4" strip of kombu seaweed
- 8 cups of warm (not hot) water

For shabu shabu

- 1 x 16-oz. pkg. of udon or rice noodles, cooked
- 1 x 16-oz. pkg. of cubed, drained, tofu, firm
- 1 peeled sliced potato, russet
- 1/2 bunch of sliced asparagus
- 1 washed, sliced leek
- 5 to 6 oz. of enoki mushrooms
- 4 oz. of sliced cremini mushrooms
- 2 heads of trimmed baby Bok choy with separated leaves
- 1 1/4 lbs. of thinly sliced brisket
- Sesame dipping sauce (see recipe 1)

Instructions:

1. Place eight cups of water (warm) in a pot. Add dried shiitake mushrooms and kombu seaweed and soak for 1/2 hour or longer. Keep the pot covered.

2. After the soaking, uncover. Bring to simmer. Remove from heat and allow to soak for five more minutes. Strain dashi and return to pot. Heat dashi to simmer.

3. Arrange meat and cut veggies and tofu on large platters. Place cooked noodles in serving bowl. Each guest gets little dishes with dipping sauces (see recipe 1), a bowl to eat from, a slotted spoon and fondue forks to dip with.

4. Bring dashi to table. Keep at simmer, do not boil. Diners add meat and veggies to pot to cook. Dip meat and veggies into sauce.

5. Add noodles to dashi pot and scoop back out into bowl for each person to enjoy, too.

16 – Rib-Eye Spinach Shabu Shabu

Windy, cold weather is the perfect time for hot pot dinners. The concept is simple. Rib-eye beef cooks nicely in the hot broth, and you can choose veggie substitutions to tailor the taste for your family or guests.

Makes 6-10 Servings

Cooking + Prep Time: 40 minutes

Ingredients:

- 8 cups of water
- 2 cups of spinach leaves, fresh
- 1 x 12-oz. container of cubed tofu, extra firm
- 2 leeks, only pale green white parts, cut in 1/2" slices
- 4 stemmed quartered mushrooms, shiitake, large
- 2 cups of bite-sized Napa cabbage cubes
- 12-16 oz. of steak, cut in 1/8" slices

Instructions:

1. Arrange meat on platter. Cover and refrigerate platter. Do the same with veggies.

2. Bring water to boil in pot, then transfer pot to stove top on table.

3. Place veggies and then meat in the pot. Swish until meat is cooked – this only takes 5-15 seconds.

4. Serve with dipping sauces (see recipe 1).

17 – Shrimp Beef Shabu Shabu

Shabu shabu is a hassle-free, impressive way to fill up your diners with food that is so belly-friendly. Being prepared at a communal table, it brings your guests together and lets them interact, even as they are cooking the meal, piece by piece.

Makes 6 Servings

Cooking + Prep Time: 1 hour 15 minutes

Ingredients:

- 2 cups of sliced mushrooms
- 1 sliced head of Napa cabbage
- 1 x 5-ounce bag of spinach, baby

- 8 ounces of halved, de-veined shrimp, large
- 8 ounces of thinly sliced beef tenderloin
- 2 slices of kombu seaweed
- 3 sliced chilies, serrano
- 1 tsp. of garlic paste
- 3 tbsp. of lemon juice, fresh
- 1/2 cup of soy sauce, low sodium
- 1/2 cup of vinegar, rice

Instructions:

1. Combine chilies, garlic paste, lemon juice, soy sauce and vinegar in small sized bowl.

2. Fill medium sauce pan 2/3 full of water. Soak kombu for 30 minutes. Arrange meat and vegetables on large platter. Remove kombu right before water starts to boil.

3. Swish ingredients in boiling broth one by one. Dip into sauce (see recipe 1).

18 – Chicken Fish Shabu Shabu

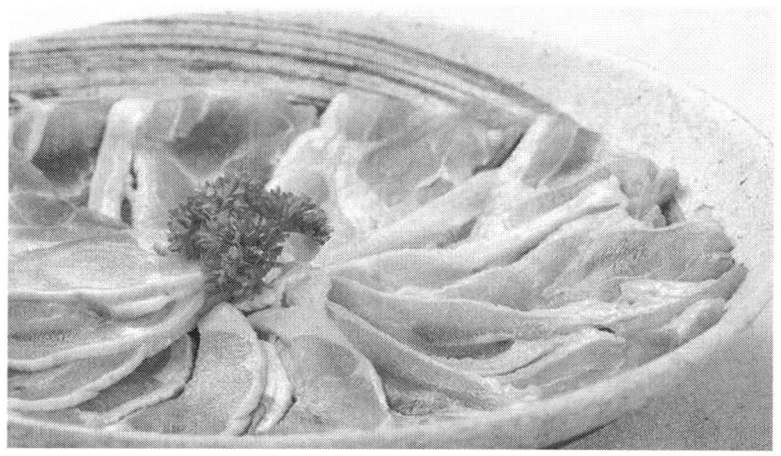

Shabu shabu is like the Japanese fondue. The food isn't cooked in oil – rather, it is cooked in hot broth. As the meal ends, you can add noodles to your broth, and it flavors the noodles with all the ingredients that came before.

Makes 6 Servings

Cooking + Prep Time: 30 minutes

Ingredients:

- 8 oz. of soaked, drained Chinese noodles
- 10 sliced green onions
- Sliced spinach, fresh

- Sliced cabbage, Chinese
- 1/2 pound of mushrooms
- 1/2 pound of cubed white fish, firm
- 6 halved chicken livers
- 1 1/2 pounds of cubed skinless, boneless chicken breasts
- 1 pound of cubed beef, lean
- 10 cups of broth, chicken

Dipping sauces – see recipe 1

- Sesame sauce
- Ponzu sauce

Instructions:

1. Heat the broth to boil on the stove. Transfer to tabletop cooker like a fondue pot. Keep the flame hot enough for the boiling to continue.

2. Each guest cooks pieces of meat and veggies to their desired doneness, and then into dipping sauce (see recipe 1).

19 – Enoki Beef Shabu Shabu

You can use meat or vegetable stock rather than dashi for your shabu shabu. The stock adds lots of flavor and it's easier to source for home cooks. Once you discover how fun shabu shabu is to make, you'll be making it often.

Makes 4-6 Servings

Cooking + Prep Time: 35 minutes

Ingredients:

- 3 cups of filtered water
- 3 cups of stock, chicken

- 4 oz. of shiitake mushrooms with removed stems
- 1 pkg. of trimmed, pulled apart enoki mushrooms
- 1 bunch of sliced green onions
- 1/4 head of chopped Napa cabbage
- 1 block of cubed tofu, firm
- 1 lb. of thinly sliced rib-eye stead

Instructions:

1. Arrange the meat and veggies on serving dishes. Set up portable burner on table.

2. Place medium pot on burner. Add water and chicken stock. Bring to simmer – do not boil.

3. Have diners add veggies and tofu. Start with the ones that will take the longest time to cook. As they become ready, diners can add their meats for 5-15 seconds.

4. Dip veggies, tofu and meat into dipping sauces (see recipe 1).

20 – Hot Pot Shabu Shabu

This is similar to other shabu shabu recipes, except that it includes tofu and fish cakes, and no meat. It's a winter dish for Japan that balances the filling ingredients with vegetables and greens.

Makes 4 Servings

Cooking + Prep Time: 25 minutes

Ingredients:

- 1 pkt. of fish cake
- 1 pkt. of fish balls, filled with roe
- 2 lbs. of thinly sliced beef
- 1 pkt. of fried tofu
- 1 pkt. of mushrooms, enoki
- 1 tbsp. of miso paste
- 1 pc. of kombu seaweed, dried
- 4 cups of water

Dipping Sauces – see recipe 1

- sesame sauce
- ponzu sauce

Instructions:

1. Fill medium pot 2/3 full of water. Add kombu. Simmer on med-low for 10 minutes or more. Remove kombu as water starts to boil. Add miso paste into broth 'til it dissolves.

2. Slice veggies into bite sized pieces. Arrange on serving platter. Place pot of boiling water on a portable burner on table.

3. Each diner cooks their veggies and beef in boiling broth, swishing to cook and then dipping in sauce (see recipe 1).

21 – Tenderloin Broccoli Shabu Shabu

This broth will become more flavorful as the veggies and meat are cooked. So, it Makes a wonderful soup at the end of the meal. Kombu can be purchased at Japanese groceries.

Makes 4 Servings

Cooking + Prep Time: 20 minutes

Ingredients:

- 4 cups of stock, chicken
- 2 shredded leaves of cabbage, Chinese

- 8 broccoli florets, small
- 2 peeled cut carrots
- 1 square of cubed tofu
- 2 cut green onions
- 4 trimmed and halved shiitake mushrooms
- 1 pound of prime beef
- 1 x 5-inch kombu sea kelp
- Ponzu Sauce – see recipe 1

Instructions:

1. Put stock and kombu in medium hot. Heat to boil, removing kombu just before the boiling starts.

2. Allow broth to simmer. Arrange meat and veggies on platters.

3. Fill fondue pat with the stock. Keep hot on a burner.

4. Each diner gets to pick up veggies and meat with fondue forks and swish in broth until cooked.

5. Veggies and meat are then dipped in sauces (see recipe 1).

22 – Shabu Shabu Vegetable Soup

Bok choy or Napa cabbage are sometimes used in lieu of Chinese broccoli in shabu shabu recipes. The soup is tasty with almost any ingredients. You'll be glad if there are leftovers, so you can have it for a meal the next day.

Makes 6-8 Servings

Cooking + Prep Time: 1 hour 25 minutes

Ingredients:

- 1 pound of washed broccoli, Chinese
- 9 ounces of sliced shiitake mushrooms

- 10 cups of water, filtered
- 5 cups of stock, vegetable
- 1 pound of tofu, firm
- 1 pound of fish balls
- Kosher salt ground pepper, as desired

Instructions:

1. Bring stock and water to boil in medium pot. Add 1 tbsp. salt. Cover and lower the heat. Allow to simmer for about an hour.

2. Add fish balls and mushrooms. Allow to simmer for five more minutes.

3. Season broth with salt pepper. Add the tofu. Allow to simmer for a few more minutes. Serve as a soup or with rice. This recipe uses the shabu shabu cooking method without the chopsticks or fondue forks.

23 – Paleo Shabu Shabu

Shabu shabu is a wonderful way to make an interactive, lively dinner. It's nutritious, too. You can eat rice, noodles, veggies and meat all in one meal. Everyone can dip in whatever they like, and the tastes are unique and delicious.

Makes 2 Servings

Cooking + Prep Time: 20 minutes

Ingredients:

- 1 large pot of chicken or vegetable broth
- Vegetables, your choice
- 1/2 pound of beef, sliced thinly
- Dipping sauces – your choice – (see recipe 1)

Instructions:

1. Boil broth in medium pot.

2. Place veggies and meat on platters.

3. Set up fondue pot on dinner table. Pour broth in fondue pot.

4. Diners can dip their veggies and sliced meat into broth to cook.

5. Serve with dipping sauce (see recipe 1).

24 – Pork Vegetable Shabu Shabu

This one pot meal is so easy, and it takes fewer than 40 minutes to bring it to the table. You can use green beans and carrots, or opt for scallions, peppers, asparagus or mushrooms.

Makes 4 Servings

Cooking + Prep Time: 35 minutes

Ingredients:

- 2/3 pot of vegetable stock
- 1/2 pound of green beans
- 1 carrots, sliced
- 12 to 16 leaves of lettuce
- 1 pound of pork loin, lean, sliced thinly

Instructions:

1. Boil stock in pan. Add veggies. Pour into fondue pot on dinner table.

2. Have guests dip their meat with chopsticks into the boiling broth.

3. Serve with your favorite dipping sauce (see recipe 1).

25 – Beef Sea Tangle Shabu Shabu

Shabu shabu is such a communal meal, since it is cooked right at the table, with people cooking their own meats and veggies. After dipping in the boiling broth to cook, the ingredients are dipped into sauces that add a great finishing taste.

Makes 4 Servings

Cooking + Prep Time: 25 minutes

Ingredients:

- 1/2 quart of water, filtered
- 1/2 quart of beef broth
- 4 inches of sea tangle, dried
- 4 mushrooms, shiitake
- 1 leek
- 7 ounces of Napa cabbage
- 1 block of tofu, firm
- 14 ounces of pork or beef, sliced thinly

Instructions:

1. Boil 2/3 pot of beef broth and water. Bring down to simmer. Move to fondue pot on table with heat source underneath it.

2. Cut block of tofu in half lengthways. Cut both halves crossways three times. Cut into bite sized pieces. Cut cabbage into bite-sized pieces, as well.

3. Slice green onion. De-stem shiitake mushrooms.

4. Arrange veggies, meat and tofu on platters.

5. Diners can dip their veggies and meat in hot broth to heat, and then into the dipping sauces (see recipe 1).

26 – Tofu Pork Shabu Shabu

Shabu shabu can be made with as many or as few ingredients as you please. This recipe doesn't have a multitude of ingredients, but they blend together so well. Incorporate some standard ingredients and add optional ingredients where you like.

Makes 4 Servings

Cooking + Prep Time: 40 minutes

Ingredients:

- 1 piece of dashi, kombu
- Enoki mushrooms with removed ends
- Halved shiitake mushrooms
- 1 pkg. of noodles, udon
- 1 cubed block of tofu, soft
- 1/4 head of chopped Napa cabbage
- 1 bunch of baby spinach
- 2 pkgs. of shabu shabu pork meat
- Water and vegetable stock
- Ponzu sauce – see recipe 1

Instructions:

1. Pour water and stock into pot at 2/3 full. Add kombu dashi into water. Allow it to sit and soak. Bring to boil, then down to simmer. Pour into fondue pot.

2. Grate veggies and place in serving bowls.

3. Slice shiitake mushrooms and remove bottoms. Cut noodles into 6-inch short pieces. Set them aside.

4. Have diners add vegetables and meat to boiling broth. Dip them in sauces (see recipe 1).

27 – Garlic Chicken Shabu Shabu

This recipe will make your dinner more fun. It Makes an interactive dinnertime treat, so people can be sociable while they cook their meats and veggies. Everyone can dip in whatever sauce they prefer.

Makes 8 Servings

Cooking + Prep Time: 1 hour 10 minutes

Ingredients:

- 6 cups of white rice, cooked
- 1/2 cup of soy sauce

- 1 tbsp. of star anise pieces
- 2-4 lbs. of chicken, sliced thinly
- 2 x 8-oz. cans of drained, rinsed, peeled, sliced water chestnuts
- 6 oz. of snow peas in pods
- 2 bunches of green onions
- 1 1/2-inch slice of peeled ginger, fresh
- 8 cloves of peeled smashed garlic
- 2 pkgs. of shitake mushrooms, dried
- 8 cups of chicken broth

Instructions:

1. Heat two cups of broth until it is warm. Soak mushrooms for 10-15 minutes. As they soak, prepare veggies and slice chicken. After the 15 minutes has passed, drain mushrooms and set them aside.

2. Place chicken, remaining stock, star anise, garlic and ginger in pot. Cover and bring it to boil.

3. Add soy sauce and mushroom liquid. When broth boils again, add mushrooms and green onions. Continue to cook while moderately boiling for five minutes.

4. Add water chestnuts and snow peas. Cover. Return to medium bowl. Remove cover and adjust heat to keep the pot boiling moderately for three or four minutes until snow peas have cooked well but are still crunchy. Skim veggies out of broth using a slotted spoon. Scatter over the top.

5. Serve 1/2 cup of rice in bottom of bowls. Have guests dip the meat and veggies in fondue pot with hot broth. Veggies take longer than meat to cook. Dip in your choice of sauce (see recipe 1).

28 – Mushroom-Noodle Shabu Shabu

This is a delicious and beautiful shabu shabu that is made with mushrooms, noodles, Napa cabbage and beef. They can be pre-assembled and then cooked when your guests or family members want to eat.

Makes 4 Servings

Cooking + Prep Time: 80 minutes

Ingredients:

- 1 pkg. of noodles, udon or ramen
- 2 green onions
- 6 ounces of bean sprouts
- 3 ounces of enoki mushrooms
- 3 1/2 ounces of beech mushrooms
- 3 shiitake mushrooms, dried
- 1 to 2 pkg. of perilla leaves
- 1 Napa cabbage
- 1 pound of beef, sliced thinly

For stock

- 2 shiitake mushrooms, dried
- 1/2 onion
- 1 large radish piece
- 15 pieces of anchovies, dried
- 1 pc. of dried kelp
- 10 cups of water

Instructions:

1. Soak the shiitake mushrooms to hydrate, in warm water.

2. Add onion, mushroom, kelp, anchovies, radish and water to pot to start the stock. Bring it to a boil. Lower immediately to simmer and allow it to remain there for at least 1/2 hour.

3. Pour stock into fondue pot or hot pot.

4. Diners should dip their veggie and meat pieces into hot stock to cook it. Then they can dip the pieces in dipping sauce (see recipe 1).

29 – Sukiyaki Shabu Shabu

You can adjust the taste of this shabu shabu by adding or reducing the amount of mirin included. The mirin is the secret to great tasting meat. The more the meat sips it, the better the aroma – and the taste, of course.

Makes 4-5 Servings

Cooking + Prep Time: 35 minutes

Ingredients:

- 4 tbsp. of mirin
- 1 1/2 pkgs. of mushrooms, champignon
- 1 mushroom, enoki
- 4 tbsp. of sugar, granulated
- 1 pkg. of tofu, firm
- 1 bunch of cabbage, Chinese
- 2 pounds of sliced meat (beef, chicken, pork)
- 1/2 pkg. of shirataki mushrooms, dry

For stock/soup

- 3 tbsp. of mirin
- 3 pkgs. of dashi stock
- 1 liter of water, filtered

Instructions:

1. Bring stock and water to boil. Mix well. The liquid of champignon pkg. can be added, too. Add sugar, mirin and soy sauce. Mix until sugar has dissolved fully.

2. Pour soup into hot pot or fondue pot.

3. Arrange veggies and meat on platters.

4. Diners will dip veggies first, then meat into hot broth to cook it.

5. Provide dipping sauces for extra taste (see recipe 1).

30 – Pork Shabu Shabu Salad

Here's something different – a shabu shabu salad. It's a great dish for summer days, when your family doesn't want to sit over boiling broth. The dressings are much the same, and they add as much flavor to a salad as they do to individual ingredients.

Makes 2 Servings

Cooking + Prep Time: 30 minutes

Ingredients:

- 2 tbsp. soy sauce
- 3 1/3 ounces dashi stock
- 1 tbsp. oil, sesame
- Shiso leaves
- 2 tsp. sugar, granulated
- 2 tbsp. sesame seeds, ground
- 1/4 medium carrot
- 2 cherry tomatoes
- 1 cucumber
- 1/4 head of lettuce
- 7 ounces of pork, sliced thinly

Instructions:

1. Julienne the lettuce, cucumber and carrots. Julienne shiso leaves, then soak in water before draining. Cut tomatoes into two to four pieces each.

2. Pour sake into boiling water. Boil pork slices. Transfer them to a bowl of cold water. Drain. Transfer veggies to plate. Top with boiled meat. Garnish using shiso leaves.

3. Grind sesame seeds. Mix with seasoning ingredients.

4. Toss lettuce and top with other veggies and meat. Serve this shabu shabu salad.

Conclusion

This shabu shabu cookbook has shown you…

How to use different ingredients to affect sweet or spicy tastes in some Japanese dishes you may have heard of, and some you have probably not heard of.

So, what can you do now?

You and your guests can enjoy Shabu shabu just as you would a fondue meal, with ingredients being cooked individually as the meal progresses. The vegetables and meats in the recipes are not written in stone, so you can substitute where you prefer. The dipping sauces are the final touch of taste for these wonderful meals.

Shabu shabu cuisine can be an interesting part of your cooking palette. These recipes will increase your knowledge about which type of ingredients will give you authentic Japanese taste.

Have fun experimenting! Enjoy the results!

Made in the USA
San Bernardino, CA
12 July 2018